You are the love I want...

LOIS WYSE

American Greetings Corporation
Cleveland, Ohio 44144

Published by American Greetings, American Road, Cleveland, Ohio 44
First printing, June, 1971. Copyright, 1971, by Lois Wyse.
Library of Congress Catalogue Card Number: 74-157555
Printed in the United States of America
An American Greetings Book

because I always have and always will

With This Ring . . .

A wedding ring is not
A true sign of marriage,
For a true sign of marriage
Cannot be touched by others.

Crossed Wires

No marriage is
A model of technical efficiency
Which is why
Marriage can work
Even though
The wires are sometimes crossed.

Playmates

I was not raised to be your mate.
So why do you remind me
Of my childhood?

Grown-up Logic

How strange it is that we insist
On asking children
What they want to be.
For how often do we ask
What it is we are?

What Time Does the 11 O'clock News Go On?

Love is not programmed like TV.
You cannot push a button and get me.
The vertical adjustment
Will not straighten all our problems,
And horizontal may just widen the gap.
So please turn off the television,
And let us see what happens
Without Ed Sullivan to watch.

The Critic

It is very difficult to judge a husband,
But so easy to criticize him.

No Better Place

This was such a lovely day,
A lovely, loving day.
The fog locked us
High above the city,
Suspended between
The walkers and the flyers.
What better place for lovers?

Thank You

You taught me how to give
The most important gift of all:
Myself to me.

Are You Confused, My Dear?

There are those who do confuse
Politics and literature,
Pride and passion,
Duty and pleasure.
Let them live with those confusions
So long as they do not blur
The differences between
Love and Like,
Man and Woman,
You and Me.

Front-page Husband

I should not like to be the wife
Of a man whose concern is
The judgment of history.

I like my tonights
Better than his tomorrows.

At Last I Am a Real Live Grown-up Person

As a child
I was forced into a mold
That equated growth and goodness
And so I felt
Growth was the proper, boresome thing to do.

      Wear white gloves
      And grow two inches.

It was not until we met and loved
That I at last did find
Growth can be a thrilling thing
When one is never forced to grow.

      I feel the brush strokes of Cézanne
      Now that I know the touch of you.

Linear Construction

There can be no happy endings
Without beginnings.
So, my dear, why wait?
Let us begin.

We are just now starting our beginning.

I Love You

E-

The Author

Lois Wyse is the author of best-selling books of
love poetry, including "Love Poems For The Very Married",
"Are You Sure You Love Me?", and "I Love You Better Now",
as well as the popular non-fiction book, "Mrs. Success".
Her articles and poems appear regularly in numerous
magazines in the United States and abroad.

Lois Wyse, her husband Marc, and their two children,
Katherine and Robert, live in Shaker Heights, Ohio.